IAN OLIO

THE INUIT OR ESKIMO?

Discover the Secrets of the People of the Arctic!

MAKE YOUR KID SMART SERIES

For Kids
Ages 3-6

This book belongs to:

....

....

It has become common to refer to the Inuit as Eskimos, but you should know they have different names for themselves. In Canada and Greenland they prefer to be called Inuit, while in Alaska they prefer the term Eskimo.

In this book we will use the term Inuit.

The Inuit people live in the cold tundra climate, in the far northern areas of Alaska, Canada, Siberia, and Greenland.

The Inuit word for home is "igloo". They learned to make warm homes out of snow and ice for the winter. For the summer they make tents from animal skin.

The Inuit traditionally got all their food by fishing and hunting. They were unable to grow their own food because of the cold climate they lived in.

They used harpoons to hunt. They ate reindeer, seal, walrus, and whale meat. Most of the meat they ate was fatty. Fat gave them energy in the cold weather.

The Inuit needed thick and warm clothing to survive cold winters. They used animal skins and furs to make clothes and blankets and stay warm.

They mainly used caribou and seal skin to make shirts, pants, boots, hats and big jackets called anoraks. They would also use polar bear, rabbit or fox fur.

Inuit women were responsible for sewing, cooking and raising the children. The men provided food and were responsible for hunting and fishing.

Did you know that a member
of the Inuit people is called
an Inuk?

The Inuit live in an area that is mostly snowy, so it has always been important to find easy forms of transportation. Most of the Inuit tribes used dogsleds and kayaks.

Can you imagine that today 89% of the total population of Greenland is Inuit? There are different Inuit groups and each group speaks its own language.

Polar bear is one of the most respected animals by the Inuit. It has several qualities that the Inuit admire: their strength, patience, speed or maternal devotion to their cubs.

Today there are only about 60,000 Inuit people in the world.

About half of them live in Alaska.

Goodbye!

Printed in Great Britain
by Amazon